BIOMIMICRY

AWESOME INNOVATIONS
INSPIRED BY
WHALES

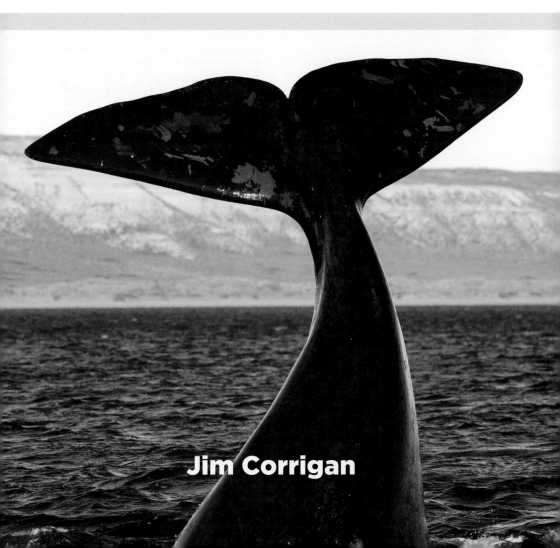

Jim Corrigan

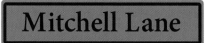

Mitchell Lane

PUBLISHERS

mitchelllane.com

2001 SW 31st Avenue
Hallandale, FL 33009

First Edition, 2021.
Author: Jim Corrigan
Designer: Ed Morgan
Editor: Sharon F. Doorasamy

Series: Biomimicry
Title: Awesome Innovations Inspired by Whales / by Jim Corrigan

Hallandale, FL : Mitchell Lane Publishers, [2021]

Library bound ISBN: 978-1-68020-613-5
eBook ISBN: 978-1-68020-614-2

Contents

1 Bumpy Fins   4

2 Gentle Giants   8

3 Filter Feeders   14

4 Precious Poop   20

5 Whale of a Future   24

What You Should Know   28

Want to be an engineer?   29
Architect? Inventor?

Glossary   30

Online Resources   31

Further Reading   31

Index   32

About the Author   32

Bumpy Fins

One day, a biologist named Frank Fish strolled through a Boston gift shop. He spotted a small statue of a humpback whale. Fish stopped to examine the whale's fins, which had strange, knobby bumps.

The bumps, called **tubercles**, made no sense to him. A whale's flippers must glide through the water, just as an airplane's wings glide through the air. Wouldn't smooth fins be better? He decided to find out.

Fish teamed up with other scholars to perform tests. Their experiments showed some fascinating results. The tubercles, they found, help humpbacks catch tiny fish.

A humpback whale is the size of a school bus. Its only hope of catching fast little fish is with sharp, sudden turns. Tubercles make those turns possible. A humpback's flippers channel water as smooth fins never could.

chapter one

Better Blades

Today, Frank Fish is president of a company called WhalePower. His company designs more efficient blades for products like ceiling fans and boat propellers. When someone finds a better way to do something, it's called **innovation**.

In 2018, Fish and his WhalePower coworkers received an honor. They were named finalists for the European Inventor Award. Their invention: a new blade for wind turbines.

Around the world, wind farms provide clean energy. The United States already has more than 60,000 wind turbines. Roughly 3,000 new turbines are built each year. The WhalePower blade will make them more efficient. It can help wind farms produce up to 20 percent more electricity.

When innovators borrow ideas from nature, it's called **biomimicry**. (*Bio* means "life" and *mimic* means "to copy.") The WhalePower team used biomimicry for their turbine blade. They copied the shape of humpback flippers.

Whales evolved from much smaller land animals. As they moved into the water, their bodies adapted to swimming. Legs became flippers. They grew a thick layer of fat, called blubber, to stay warm. With plenty of food and less gravity, whales reached tremendous sizes.

We are only beginning to understand the importance of whales in nature, and in biomimicry.

FUN FACT

Want to know a whale's age?
Check its earwax. Scientists count the bands of earwax to estimate a whale's age. It's a lot like counting a tree's rings.

Gentle Giants

Humans and whales share a complex history. In ancient times, coastal humans hunted whales for food. A single kill fed entire villages. No part of the animal was wasted. Villagers lit lamps with whale oil and carved the bones into tools.

By 1750, whale hunting had become big business. Fleets of whaling ships sailed the world's oceans, harvesting valuable whale oil. Some species started to become scarce.

Demand for whale oil surged in the 1800s. Whalers used faster ships and deadly harpoon guns. But the worst was yet to come. More whales would be hunted in the early 1900s than in the previous four centuries combined.

If not for a replacement fuel called petroleum, whales might have been hunted to extinction.

The United States outlawed whaling in 1971, and many other nations soon did too. (Norway and Japan remain notable exceptions.) Some native peoples are permitted to hunt whales for food, as their ancestors did.

The ban on whaling allowed many species to recover. Hunting had shrunk the humpback population by 90 percent. Today, there are 80,000 humpbacks. They no longer appear on the list of threatened species.

Whale oil was once used for everything from gas lamps and candles to detergents and perfume.

The North Atlantic right whale is a different story. Right whales are slow and placid. Hunters found them easy targets and nearly killed them all. Fewer than 500 North Atlantic right whales exist today.

Whaling's bloody days are over, but whales still die in accidents. They are struck by ships or tangled in fishing nets.

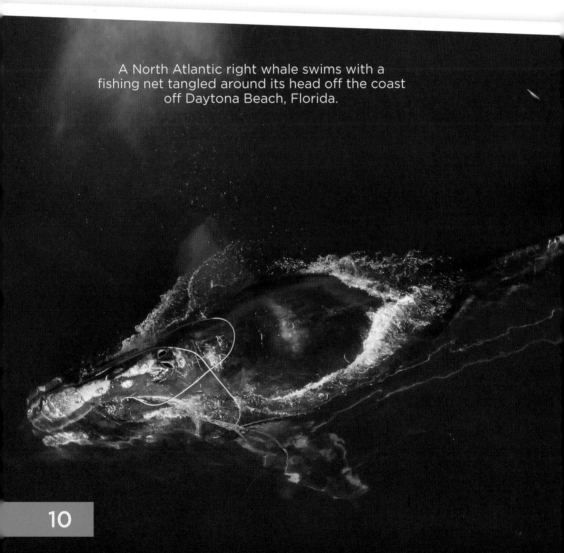

A North Atlantic right whale swims with a fishing net tangled around its head off the coast off Daytona Beach, Florida.

Scientists from the National Oceanic and Atmospheric Administration successfully remove the netting after approaching the young whale.

Pollution is another threat. In 2019, a 10-year-old sperm whale washed up in Scotland with 220 pounds (100 kilograms) of trash in its belly. Scientists estimate that 8 million tons of plastic end up in the ocean every year.

New Beginning

Many nations now see whales as a precious resource, worthy of protection and study. A science writer named Janine Benyus goes one step further. She believes whales can also help us make a better tomorrow.

In 1997, Benyus wrote a book entitled *Biomimicry: Innovation Inspired by Nature.* She pointed out an interesting fact about many plants and animals, including whales. These creatures have been around for much longer than humans. They have developed some amazing survival tricks.

Whales, for example, are expert navigators. They can travel vast distances in dark water without straying off course. Scientists marvel at this feat.

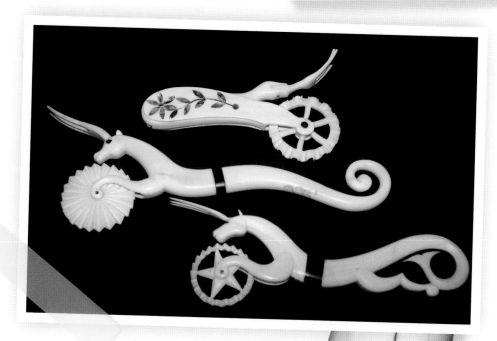

FUN FACT

Sailors on whaling ships passed the time by carving whale bones and teeth. Their artwork was known as scrimshaw. Sailors carved toys, utensils, and pictures.

Filter Feeders

The blue whale
is the largest animal in the world.
Dinosaurs, including the mighty T. rex, would look puny by comparison. A blue whale's tongue weighs as much as an elephant. Its heart? As much as a car. Even its blood vessels are wide enough for you to swim through.

Yet for all its size, the blue whale has no teeth. Its favorite food is **krill**, a tiny, shrimp-like animal. An adult blue whale can eat 40 million krill each day. It scoops up a mouthful and then pushes out the water through bristles called **baleen**. Rows of baleen act as a filter, holding back the tasty krill.

Researchers at the University of South Australia mimicked whales to build a better water filter. The Baleen Filter makes clean drinking water. It removes pollutants without the need for chemicals, and it is self-cleaning. The inventors received numerous awards.

Going the Distance

The blue whale's enormous appetite means it must travel. Otherwise, it would run out of krill. In the North Pacific, blue whales spend their summers off the U.S. and Canadian coast. For winter they head south, going as far as Costa Rica. Their two-month journey covers thousands of miles.

We navigate on long trips with maps, GPS, and road signs. Whales use other methods. They have **bio sonar**, which helps them "see" using sound waves instead of light. Some researchers suspect that whales also sense Earth's magnetic field. The planet's magnetic field is not consistent. It has many folds and wrinkles. Evidence suggests that whales follow these magnetic creases like highways.

Whale song appears to be another important navigation tool. The low-frequency moans can travel for thousands of miles. Whales may use their songs to keep each other on course. Members of the same **pod** will turn in unison, despite being many miles apart. Males also sing complex songs to attract females.

A mother and her calf swim in waters near Maui, Hawaii.

Whales sometimes pop their heads above the surface to have a look around. Scientists call it "spy-hopping." The whale tilts its huge body vertically and then flaps its tail. It's a bit like treading water. A typical spy-hop lasts 15 to 30 seconds, giving the whale a good view of its surroundings.

Precious Poop

In 2012, an English boy was walking on the beach with his father. The boy, Charlie Naysmith, found a strange rock. They took the rock home and went online to identify it.

To Charlie's surprise, it wasn't a rock at all. He had found whale poop. And it turned out to be more than just ordinary whale poop. Charlie had found a very rare whale excretion called ambergris. The caramel-colored chunk, weighing just over a pound, was worth more than $60,000.

Ambergris forms after a sperm whale swallows a squid beak or other hard object. A greasy wax builds up around the beak to keep it from doing any harm. Eventually, the whale expels the wax ball along with other waste.

Fresh ambergris smells like poop. But after floating in the ocean for a few years it starts to smell better. By the time a clump of ambergris washes ashore, it is delightfully fragrant. Perfume makers pay top dollar for it.

Some nations, including the United States, ban the sale of ambergris. They fear that greedy treasure hunters might harm sperm whales, which are a threatened species.

In 2013, the Swiss company Firmenich learned to mass produce fake ambergris. Their plant-based product costs much less than actual whale poop. Today, only the most extravagant perfumes contain real ambergris.

chapter four

Whale Pump

In recent years, scientists have realized that whale waste can help with climate change. Carbon dioxide is the main greenhouse gas. Whale poop triggers an important process that pulls carbon dioxide from the air. Scientists call this process the "whale pump."

Whales feed in deep, dark waters, eating tons of nutritious krill and fish. When whales come to the sunlit surface for air, they also poop. A plume of whale poop can run the length of three school buses. It's packed with nutrients, which feed tiny floating plants called **phytoplankton**.

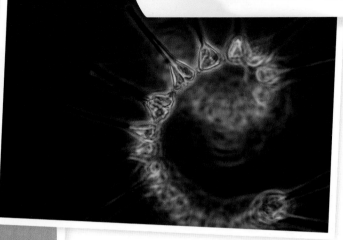

Phytoplankton are a lot like land-based plants. With sunlight, they soak up carbon dioxide and give off the oxygen we breathe. Phytoplankton in the ocean captures four times more carbon dioxide than does the Amazon rainforest.

By eating and pooping, whales pump rich nutrients from the dark depths up to the sunny surface. They fertilize the shallow water where phytoplankton grow.

The whale pump can help us fight climate change. Today, the world has about 1.3 million whales. Before industrial whaling, there were 4 to 5 million. Scientists say that if we can get back to those levels, whales would help remove 1.7 billion tons of carbon dioxide each year.

Whale of a Future

Long ago, coal miners used canaries to detect dangerous gas. The little birds were sensitive to changes in the air. If a canary got sick, the miners knew it was time to go.

Plants and animals that warn us of danger are called **sentinel** species. Whales are a sentinel species of the ocean. When their behavior changes, scientists know there is a problem.

Seas around the world are warming from climate change. Nowhere is this more evident than in the Gulf of Maine. The gulf has always been a favorite feeding spot for whales, until lately. In 2011, scientists noticed that fewer whales were visiting the gulf. Since then, the Gulf of Maine has come under intense scientific scrutiny.

Today, we know that the gulf's whale population is at an all-time low. We also know that climate change is ravaging the gulf. Studies show that the Gulf of Maine is warming faster than 99 percent of the world's ocean surface.

Scientists continue to watch this flashpoint of climate change. They hope to find clues for slowing the damage, both in the gulf and around the globe.

Gulf of
Maine

chapter five

Medical Mystery

Cancer is a common disease in many species, including humans. It occurs when abnormal cells grow into tumors. We understand a great deal about the disease, but many mysteries remain. One of them involves whales.

Two key risks for cancer are size and age. The larger and older a creature is, the more likely it is to get cancer. Whales are the largest creatures on the planet. They can live to 90 and beyond. Logically, whales should fall victim to cancer, but they hardly ever do. Cancer in whales is super rare.

In 2019, a team of scientists decided to find out why. They mapped the **genome** of a humpback whale. It showed an abundance of anti-cancer genes, far more than in other animals.

The team believes that whales evolved these genes by necessity. It was the only way they could survive as giants. This discovery is an important first step. Someday, whale genes might yield answers for preventing cancer in humans.

Biomimicry is the act of copying nature to solve human problems. Natural solutions do not harm the environment. With biomimicry, people in science and business are finding tomorrow's ideas today.

Whale of a Future

Salt has played an important role in research.

For their cancer study, researchers took small skin samples from a humpback named Salt. New England whale watchers have known of Salt since 1975. White dots on her dorsal fin look like a sprinkle of salt. Over the years, she has given birth to at least 13 calves and is now a grandmother.

Etch-A-Sketch is Salt's granddaughter.

What You Should Know

Whales can travel thousands of miles without going off course, and they call to each other over great distances.

One company mimicked humpback flippers for a more efficient wind turbine blade. Another company made a self-cleaning water filter by mimicking the mouths of baleen whales.

A special kind of whale poop called ambergris is used in some perfumes. Many perfume makers now use an artificial version of ambergris.

Whales do not get cancer. Ongoing studies of whale genes might help humans avoid the disease.

The smart ideas that come from biomimicry have an extra benefit. They are safe for the environment.

Want to be an engineer? Architect? Inventor?

1. **Take math** and **science** classes

2. **Enroll in art** and **design** classes

3. **Attend STEM** camps and programs

4. **Visit nature preserves** and **parks** to observe nature at work

5. **Keep a journal** or a **blog** of your observations

6. **Enter science fairs** and **competitions**

7. **Check out books** on **biomimicry** from your school and public library

8. **Visit natural history museums** and **science centers**

9. **Check your community's calendar** for talks by **science** and **technology experts**

10. **Volunteer for citizen science events** like **bird counts**, **water sample collection**, and **weather reporting**

Glossary

baleen
A filter-feeder system in the mouths of some whales

bio sonar
Method of locating objects based on the echo they return; also called echolocation

biomimicry
Borrowing ideas from nature

genome
All the inheritable traits of an organism

innovation
To create or improve an object or method

krill
Small crustaceans that are food for certain whales

phytoplankton
Microscopic plant-like organisms that live in water

pod
A social group of whales

sentinel
A person or thing that stands watch

tubercle
A round bump on bone or the body's surface

Online Resources

Visit the Conservationist for Kids webpage
www.dec.ny.gov/education/40248.html for more information about: Biomimicry, Green Chemistry, Green Schools, and Sustainability

Check out the Ask Nature website
www.asknature.org

Listen to Janine Benyus talk about biomimicry
www.ted.com/speakers/janine_benyus

Learn more about citizen science projects
www.nationalgeographic.org/idea/citizen-science-projects

Enjoy the podcast 30 Animals That Made Us Smarter
www.bbc.co.uk/programmes/w13xttw7

Search YouTube for videos on biomimicry

Visit www.uspto.gov/kids/Biomimicry.pdf

Learn mind-blowing facts about the enormous blue whale
kids.nationalgeographic.com/animals/mammals/blue-whale/

Further Reading

Becker, Helaine, and Alex Ries. *Zoobots: Wild Robots Inspired by Real Animals*. Tonawanda, NY: Kids Can Press, 2014.

Koontz, Robin. *Nature-Inspired Contraptions*. North Mankato, MN: Rourke Educational Media, 2018.

Mann, Janet, ed. *Deep Thinkers: Inside the Minds of Whales, Dolphins, and Porpoises*. Chicago: University of Chicago Press, 2017.

Pyenson, Nick. *Spying on Whales: The Past, Present, and Future of Earth's Most Awesome Creatures*. New York: Penguin Books, 2018.

Index

ambergris	20–21, 28
Benyus, Janine	12
cancer	26–27, 28
Fish, Frank	4-6
Gulf of Maine	25
Naysmith, Charlie	20
scrimshaw	13
whale pump	22–23
whale song	16
whaling	8-10, 23

About the Author

Jim Corrigan has been writing nonfiction for more than 20 years. He holds degrees from Penn State and Johns Hopkins. Jim became a fan of biomimicry while working on a book about airplanes. He currently lives near Philadelphia.